YOUR KNOWLEDGE HAS VALUE

- We will publish your bachelor's and master's thesis, essays and papers

- Your own eBook and book - sold worldwide in all relevant shops

- Earn money with each sale

Upload your text at www.GRIN.com
and publish for free

Bibliographic information published by the German National Library:

The German National Library lists this publication in the National Bibliography; detailed bibliographic data are available on the Internet at http://dnb.dnb.de .

This book is copyright material and must not be copied, reproduced, transferred, distributed, leased, licensed or publicly performed or used in any way except as specifically permitted in writing by the publishers, as allowed under the terms and conditions under which it was purchased or as strictly permitted by applicable copyright law. Any unauthorized distribution or use of this text may be a direct infringement of the author s and publisher s rights and those responsible may be liable in law accordingly.

Imprint:

Copyright © 2015 GRIN Verlag, Open Publishing GmbH
Print and binding: Books on Demand GmbH, Norderstedt Germany
ISBN: 9783668296954

This book at GRIN:

http://www.grin.com/en/e-book/339907/the-wto-dispute-of-boeing-and-airbus

Irina Düsseldorf

The WTO Dispute of Boeing and Airbus

GRIN Publishing

GRIN - Your knowledge has value

Since its foundation in 1998, GRIN has specialized in publishing academic texts by students, college teachers and other academics as e-book and printed book. The website www.grin.com is an ideal platform for presenting term papers, final papers, scientific essays, dissertations and specialist books.

Visit us on the internet:

http://www.grin.com/

http://www.facebook.com/grincom

http://www.twitter.com/grin_com

Assignment

The WTO – Dispute of Boeing and Airbus

Study program: Master of Business Administration (MBA)

Executive summary

This assignment gives a general overview of the large civil aircraft market, by presenting the leaders: Airbus and Boeing. Further, the historical backgrounds were analyzed: The dispute has begun since Airbus was created in 1965, specifically to drive the US competitor Boeing out of the market.

Based on this thesis, the assignment examines the duopoly-position considering the economic backgrounds. A number of key issues arise especially from Boeing's side. Boeing lost his dominant role on the market. Furthermore, Airbus delivered very high innovative technological standards, by keeping the costs low. It did not take long time until Boeing has responded by blaming Airbus to get subsidies from the government.

All this led to the biggest dispute in history and has been a particular challenge for the World Trade Organization (WTO).

The results of this assignment point out, that there are new entrants on the aircraft market, for example China and Russia. Instead of negotiating for years about subsidies, Airbus and Boeing should concentrate on improving their technological standards. Another idea of the author is to start a cooperation between the parties. The exchange of the Know-How would lead the companies to the top and no competitor could ever overcome the high barriers to entry of the aircraft market.

The best way to summing up, is to say, that it is not a competition between aircraft industries, it is a competition between the world's largest governments: The European Union and the United States.

Table of contents

Executive summary...II

Table of contents.. III

List of abbreviations IV

List of tables V

1   Introduction... 1

2   The large civil aircraft market 2

    2.1   Boeing.. 2

    2.2   Airbus 3

    2.3   Comparing Airbus and Boeing 4

3   The competition between Airbus and Boeing... 5

    3.1   The history 5

    3.2   Economic characteristic of the aircraft industrie 6

4   The Airbus and Boeing dispute in the WTO 8

    4.1   The WTO and the General Agreement on Tariffs and Trade 8

    4.2   The lawsuit.. 9

    4.3   Current situation 9

5   Results and conclusion 11

List of literature XIII

List of abbreviations

A320	Airbus A320 aircraft family
A380	Airbus A380 aircraft family
bn	billion
EU	European Union
LCA	Large Civil Aircraft
R&D	Research and Development
US	United States
WTO	World Trade Organization
737	Boeing 737 aircraft family

List of tables

Table 1: Airbus and Boeing by comparison 4

1 INTRODUCTION

For many years Airbus and Boeing compete for supremacy. Considering that Airbus and Boeing were the largest companies on the Large Civil Aircraft (LCA) market, the competition became national and government-affiliated. This was the beginning of the dispute between the European Communities and the United States over subsidiaries given to the particular organizations.

The first chapter of the assignment gives an overview of the aircraft companies Airbus and Boeing as well as of the LCA market, in order to place the companies in the further context.

The next part of this assignment examines the history of the companies at issue and how competition within the LCA industry brought about the dispute. The author decided to have a closer look on the economic effect of the competition between Airbus and Boeing on the LCA market, assuming it might be one of the reasons for the big dispute.

Chapter 4 introduces the international agreements relevant to the WTO - dispute as well as current negotiations in the WTO concerning the compliance over subsidies.

The main target of this assignment is to figure out why the WTO dispute last for years and why there is no prospect of an end. Further information on potential solutions is given in chapter 5, in the conclusion-part of the assignment.

2 THE LARGE CIVIL AIRCRAFT MARKET

In 1975 all airlines became largely free to buy from any producer, consequently the large civil aircraft market expanded to a worldwide basis. The aforementioned market includes only passenger aircraft for use by airlines. There is also military aircraft, small aircraft, helicopters and others, but the main aircraft in the aerospace market are jets.[1] It is interesting to consider that only two large companies are competing on this market: The Boeing Company and The Airbus Group. The following two chapters give a closer look on these companies.

2.1 BOEING

Founded in 1916 in the Puget Sound region of Washington State, Boeing became a leading producer of military and commercial aircraft. Boeing's largest success came with the jet age. In 1959 Boeing received aid by military resources and technology, which was developed under favorable contracts for the Pentagon.[2] After the big merger with McDonnell Douglas in 1997 and other acquisitions with small companies, Boeing became the world's leading aerospace company.

In present times, Boeing is headquartered in Chicago and employs more than 165,000 people across the United States and in more than sixty-five countries. Boeing's customers include airlines and allied government customers. The company is designing, assembling and supporting two business units:

1. Boeing Commercial Airplanes
2. Boeing Defense, Space & Security

It is interesting to consider, that more than ten thousand Boeing-built commercial jetliners are in service worldwide, which is nearly forty-eight percent of the world fleet.[3]

---

[1] William G. Shepherd and Joanna M. Shepherd, *The Economics of Industrial Organization* (Illinois: Waveland Press, Inc., 2004), 296.
[2] Ibid.
[3] "Boeing in Brief," *Boeing*, accessed May 26, 2015, http://www.boeing.com/company/general-info/index.page#/overview.

In the year 2014, Boeing generated the revenue of 90,8 bn US dollars, 42,3 bn US dollars derived solely from commercial aircraft. Historically, seventy percent of commercial airplane revenue historically comes from customers outside the United States.

2.2 AIRBUS

Founded in 1965 Airbus has never stopped to improve its enormous product line, which is comprised of families of aircraft ranging from hundred to more than five hundred seats. Airbus' family aircraft breaks down in three types: The passenger aircraft, Airbus corporate jets and freighter aircraft. Considering the fact, that the Airbus is the producer and marketer of the largest airplane worldwide, the A380, the company is also the second largest commercial aircraft worldwide.[4]

The aircraft manufacturing company Airbus SAS is the subsidiary of the Airbus Group SE, originally formed as the European Aeronomic Defence and Space Company (EADS), which is a European multinational aerospace and defense corporation. The company employs more than 73,000 people. While headquartered in Toulouse, France, Airbus has expanded upon its strong European roots to move forward on an international scale with subsidiaries in the USA, China, Japan, India and the Middle East. Final assembly production is based at Toulouse, France; Hamburg, Germany; Seville, Spain and since 2008, as a joint venture in Tianjin, China.[5]

In the year of 2014, the Airbus Group generated the highest revenue from activities in Asia / Pacific with 19,379 million euro, followed by North America with a revenue of 9,731 million euro.[6]

---

[4] "Making Flight possible," *Airbus*, accessed June 1, 2015, http://www.airbus.com/company/.
[5] Ibid.
[6] „Investors & Shareholders," *Airbus Group*, accessed May 24, 2015,
   http://www.airbusgroup.com/int/en/investors-shareholders.html.

2.3 COMPARING AIRBUS AND BOEING

Although Boeing has more market share than Airbus and higher revenue reported in the fiscal year 2014, Airbus has more orders and deliveries for their best-seller-aircraft family A320 than Boeing for its 737 family, until 2014, according to the table 1 below.

Table 1: Airbus and Boeing by comparison[7][8][9][10]

	AIRBUS SAS	BOEING
Entity	Subsidiary of Airbus Group	Public
Founded	1965 in Toulouse, France	1916 in Washington
Headquarter	Toulouse, France	Chicago, USA
Industry	Aerospace	Aerospace, Defense, Space & Security
Revenue (commercial airplanes)	42,3 bn (2014)	60,0 bn (2014)
Employees (commercial airplanes)	More than 73,000	More than 165,000
Slogan	Leading aircraft manufacturer	Build something better
Orders until 2014	10,934 (A320 - family)	9,589 (737 – family)
Deliveries until 2014	6,201 (A320 - family)	5419 (737 – family)
Unfilled until 2014	4,733 (A320 - family)	4,170 (737 – family)

---

[7] "Boeing in Brief."
[8] "Making Flight possible."
[9] "Investors & Shareholders."
[10] "Interactive Analyst Center," last modified April 23, 2015, http://apps.indigotools.com/IR/IAC/?Ticker=BA&Exchange=NYSE#.

3 THE COMPETITION BETWEEN AIRBUS AND BOEING

The Boeing Aircraft Company was the dominant US aircraft producer during and after World War II. From numerous competitors in 1945, the industry narrowed down to just two main rivals: Boeing and Airbus.[11]

3.1 THE HISTORY

After Boeing noticed the great success of Airbus in the early seventies, it started to involve Airbus in their own projects, in order to stop Airbus' in-house development. Boeing's approach to cooperate with Airbus was a big failure and the beginning of the world's biggest dispute. Airbus refused the suggested cooperation and continued to work on innovative aircraft. Consequently Boeing blamed Airbus infringing a US patent by using the same airplane wings.[12] Due to Airbus' innovative technology, the implementing of the matrix – management and the fact that Boeing did not use the competitive advantages of the "barriers to entry"[13], Airbus receive accesse to the large US market in 1978. In a nutshell, Airbus signed the first contract with the American Eastern airline on leasing twenty-three airplanes and offered them a value-added service by sharing their training costs caused by the implementing of the delivered Airbus machines. The United States International Trade Commission (USITC) immediately started an investigation on this agreement.[14]

From all this it follows that there has been few cases of unfair tactics directed specifically at Boeing, yet the US Company constantly insists unfair governmental backing and favoritism for Airbus.[15] In the meantime Airbus continued to improve its technological standards and keep costs and prices low. This pressure forced also Boeing

---

[11] Shepherd and Shepherd, *The Economics of Industrial Organization,* 295.
[12] Andreas Schmidt, "Die Entwicklung der Flugzeugindustrie auf nationaler und betribelicher Eben – divergierende Strategien und Innovationskonzepte und ihre organisatorische Realisierung," in *Flugzeughersteller zwischen globalem Wettbewerb und internationaler Kooperation: Der Einfluß von Organisationsstrukturen auf die Wettbewerbsfähigkeit von Hochtechnologie-Unternehmen* (Berlin: edition sigma, 1997), 200-203.
[13] Ivan L. Pitt and John R. Norsworthy, *Economics of the U.S. Commercial Airline Industry: Productivity, Technology and Regulation: Transportation Research, Economics and Policy* (New York: Springer Science, 1999), 93-94.
[14] Schmidt, *"Flugzeughersteller zwischen globalem Wettbewerb,"* 204-205.
[15] Shepherd and Shepherd, *The Economics of Industrial Organization,* 295-297.

to improve its efficiency and innovation. Finally, both companies embarked on multi-billion dollar investments into the development of new aircraft, further raising the stakes. Other aircraft manufacturers were no longer able to compete successfully on the market, consequently they were driven out consequently.[16] Because of this, in 2002, Boeing and Airbus were the largest competitors on the aircraft market and remain in this position to this date.

3.2 ECONOMIC CHARACTERISTIC OF THE AIRCRAFT INDUSTRIE

With respect to Economics, there are different difficulties in entering and sustaining on the LCA – market.

- Duopolistic market

Airbus and Boeing are very dependent on the price decisions of its sole competitor.

- High barriers to market entry

The capital requirements for entry to the aircraft market are very high because of scale economies, industry size and R&D needs.[17] Economic recessions, oil price shocks, risk caused by new technology as well as difficulties in predicting demand many years ahead, make aircraft purchase unreliable. Sales in the aircraft industry often involve complex financing and parts-supply deals negotiated between the airlines and the producers.[18]

- Falling exchange rates

Special about the aircraft market is that all aircraft sales are invoiced in the US dollar - currency. Falling exchange rates between the euro and the US dollar exacerbate the risk not being able to cover the costs.

- National security

---

[16] Schmidt, *"Flugzeughersteller zwischen globalem Wettbewerb,"* 150.
[17] Shepherd and Shepherd, *The Economics of Industrial Organization,* 296.
[18] Pitt and Norsworthy, *Economics of the U.S. Commercial Airline Industry,* 94-95.

3 The competition between Airbus and Boeing

Connections with foreign government are important because they are often involved in purchase decisions by foreign airlines.[19]

---

[19] Shepherd and Shepherd, *The Economics of Industrial Organization*, 296.

4 THE AIRBUS AND BOEING DISPUTE IN THE WTO

One of the most time consuming and expensive trade disputes in WTO history started in 2004, concerning the conflict over subsidies, which had persisted between the European Community and Airbus as well as between the US communities and Boeing.[20]

4.1 THE WTO AND THE GENERAL AGREEMENT ON TARIFFS AND TRADE

The WTO was established in Marrakesh, Morocco in 1995 and has replaced the General Agreements on Tariffs and Trade (GATT), the organization that supervised the multilateral trading system. The WTO counts 161 members from all over the world, including the EU with its twenty-eight member states and the United States.[21] The WTO defines Dispute Settlements Gateways (DSG) as follows: "Dispute settlement is the central pillar of the multilateral trading system, and the WTO's unique contribution to the stability of the global economy [...]. The priority is to settle disputes, through consultation if possible [...]. Most of the rest disputes have either been notified as settled "out of court" or remain in a prolonged consultation phase — some since 1995."[22] The 1979 GATT Tokyo round of multilateral trade negotiations produced a plurilateral agreement on Trade in Civil Aircraft, the so-called "Aircraft Agreement". It was intended to eliminate a specific set of aircraft-related tariffs while also encouraging signatory states to make their civil aircraft purchasing decisions in accordance with commercial and technological, rather than nationalistic interests. In 1995 the "Aircraft Agreement" was recast and inserted to the new WTO Charter, as Annex 4.[23] Countries, which should enhance their presence in the aircraft manufacturing market, such as Brazil, China, India and Russia, did not sign the agreement.[24]

---

[20] Brian F. Havel and Gabriel S. Sanchez, *The Principles and Practice of International Aviation Law* (New York: Cambridge, 2014), 384 – 385.
[21] "Members and Observes," *World Trade Organization*, accessed May 2, 2015, https://www.wto.org/english/thewto_e/whatis_e/tif_e/org6_e.htm.
[22] "Understanding the WTO: Settling Disputes," *World Trade Organization*, accessed May 2, 2015, https://www.wto.org/english/thewto_e/whatis_e/tif_e/disp1_e.htm.
[23] Ibid.
[24] Havel and Sanchez, *The Principles and Practice of International Aviation Law,* 384.

4.2 THE LAWSUIT

The United States initiated the dispute resolution process, blaming the EU to provide subsidies to Airbus, such as loans at no interest or below-market interest rate as well as European and government Investment Bank grants. The EU responded, claiming the European Communities has suffered damage due to unfair and partial competition from Boeing. Furthermore, the EU alleged that Boeing received tax benefits for relocating its headquarters as well as received indirect subsidies in the form of R&D contracts with the National Aeronautics and Space Administration (NASA) and the Department of Defense.[25]

After years of negotiating in the WTO, several agreements were made to avoid subsidies and provide the parties with useful tools to resolve the dispute.

4.3 CURRENT SITUATION

Eleven years later, the United States and the EU parties still negotiate about subsidies. The WTO has spent significant time and resources to find a solution for this dispute. But instead of using the information received through the WTO process to negotiate an agreement about eliminating subsidies, the parties continue to allege that the other has failed to comply with WTO rules. Taking for instance Boeing's homepage: "For more than 40 years European governments have heavily subsidized Airbus. They paid 100 percent of the development costs for early Airbus products, and today Airbus still receives one-third of the billions of dollars needed to develop new commercial airplanes. […]. As a result of such substantial and ongoing assistance from European governments, Airbus has been able to capture half of the global airplane market, with significant negative impact on America's aerospace industry."[26] In contrast to this statement EU notified the WTO in December 2011, that it has taken appropriate steps to bring its measures fully into conformity with its WTO obligations and had removed all subsidies and adverse effects.[27] In February 2015, the EU complaint to the WTO,

---

[25] "Department of Commerce," *NASA*, accessed May 3, 2015, http://history.nasa.gov/presrep98/doc.html.
[26] Impact of Illegal European Subsidies on the U.S. Aerospace Indurstry," *Boeing*, accessed 14 May, 2015, http://www.boeing.com/company/key-orgs/government-operations/wto.page.
[27] "Members and Observes."

4 The Airbus and Boeing dispute in the WTO

this time on tax breaks the state of Washington recently enacted to attract new investment by aerospace companies in the state.[28] The best way to summing up the current situation is to say, that it is a never-ending story of the largest competitors in the aircraft industry.

---

[28] „Intercative Analyst Center."

5 Results and Conclusion

According to the special economic characteristics of the aircraft industry it is almost impossible to enter the LCA market. The author has mentioned different issues making the aircraft industry a duopolistic market. In the first place the high barriers to market entry and the high prices: the development of wide - body aircraft can cost up to 10 Million euros and will not be funded by private capital providers if the manufacturer is not already established in the market. It is also debatable whether the market demand is high enough to finance the development of more aircraft. All this leads to the current situation on the LCA market. The main manufacturing of wide-body aircraft is divided between the two: the United States and the EU.

As described in chapter 4, the influence of the respective government subsidies caused the dispute in the WTO. The organization is still trying to eliminate the subsidization of Boeing and Airbus. But, considering how much more expensive large aircraft will be without subsidies; it is better not to eliminate but rather to limit the subsidies. The author has the opinion that governmental influence is particularly pronounced in the aircraft industry. While Boeing has growing up largely absent direct government aid, Airbus got government aid since the very beginning. Under these circumstances it is impossible to change European as well as American tradition and philosophy.

A possible solution could be a private negotiation between the United States and the EU, outside the WTO. They could do a regular exchange of information, discussing their different types of subsidies and maybe finding a limitation for each form of subsidy.

According to the second chapter of this assignment both parties have a high market share and very high revenues, what is stopping them to cooperate? It is not efficient digging around in the past. It is better to focus on innovative technology and future of the industry. During the dispute between Airbus and Boeing, competitors from China, Russia, Japan and Canada were growing stronger.

List of literature

Airbus. "Making Flight possible." Accessed June 1, 2015. http://www.airbus.com/company/.

Airbusgroup. „Investors & Shareholders." Accessed May 24, 2015. http://www.airbusgroup.com/int/en/investors-shareholders.html.

Boeing. "Interactive Analyst Center." Last modified April 23, 2015. http://apps.indigotools.com/IR/IAC/?Ticker=BA&Exchange=NYSE#.

Boeing. "Impact of Illegal European Subsidies on the U.S. Aerospace Indurstry." Accessed 14 May, 2015. http://www.boeing.com/company/key-orgs/government-operations/wto.page.

Boeing. "Boeing in Brief." Accessed May 26, 2015. http://www.boeing.com/company/general-info/index.page#/overview.

Havel, Brian F., and Gabriel S. Sanchez. *The Principles and Practice of International Aviation Law.* New York: Cambridge, 2014.

Pitt, Ivan L., and John R. Norsworthy. *Economics of the U.S. Commercial Airline Industry: Productivity, Technology and Regulation: Transportation Research, Economics and Policy.* New York: Springer Science, 1999.

NASA. "Department of Commerce." Accessed May 3, 2015. http://history.nasa.gov/presrep98/doc.html

Schmidt, Andreas. "Die Entwicklung der Flugzeugindustrie auf nationaler und betribelicher Eben – divergierende Strategien und Innovationskonzepte und ihre organisatorische Realisierung." In *Flugzeughersteller zwischen globalem Wettbewerb und internationaler Kooperation: Der Einfluß von Organisationsstrukturen auf die Wettbewerbsfähigkeit von Hochtechnologie-Unternehmen,* 76-215. Berlin: edition sigma, 1997.

Shepherd, William G., and Joanna M. Shepherd, *The Economics of Industrial Organization.* Illinois: Waveland Press, Inc., 2004.

List of literature

World Trade Organization. "Members and Observes." Accessed May 2, 2015. https://www.wto.org/english/thewto_e/whatis_e/tif_e/org6_e.htm.

World Trade Organization. "Understanding the WTO: Settling Disputes." Accessed May 2, 2015. https://www.wto.org/english/thewto_e/whatis_e/tif_e/disp1_e.htm.

YOUR KNOWLEDGE HAS VALUE

- We will publish your bachelor's and master's thesis, essays and papers

- Your own eBook and book - sold worldwide in all relevant shops

- Earn money with each sale

Upload your text at www.GRIN.com and publish for free